nosaur eagle forest
queen planet square
ountain music rabbit
er octopus girl pond
sunny donkey hotel
candle socks kitten
tiger mitten number
niform violin spring
tor x-ray doll cheese
tue doctor elephant
e four orange zebra

ISBN 978-1-84135-642-6

Copyright © 2012 Award Publications Limited
Illustrated by Andy Peters
with additional artwork by Angie Hewitt

All rights reserved. No part of this publication may be
reproduced or utilized in any form or by any means electronic or
mechanical, including photocopying, recording, or by any information
storage and retrieval system now known or hereafter invented,
without the prior written permission of the publisher.

First published 2012

Published by Award Publications Limited,
The Old Riding School, The Welbeck Estate,
Worksop, Nottinghamshire, S80 3LR

www.awardpublications.co.uk

12 1

Printed in Malaysia

My First 1000 Words

Award Publications

My body

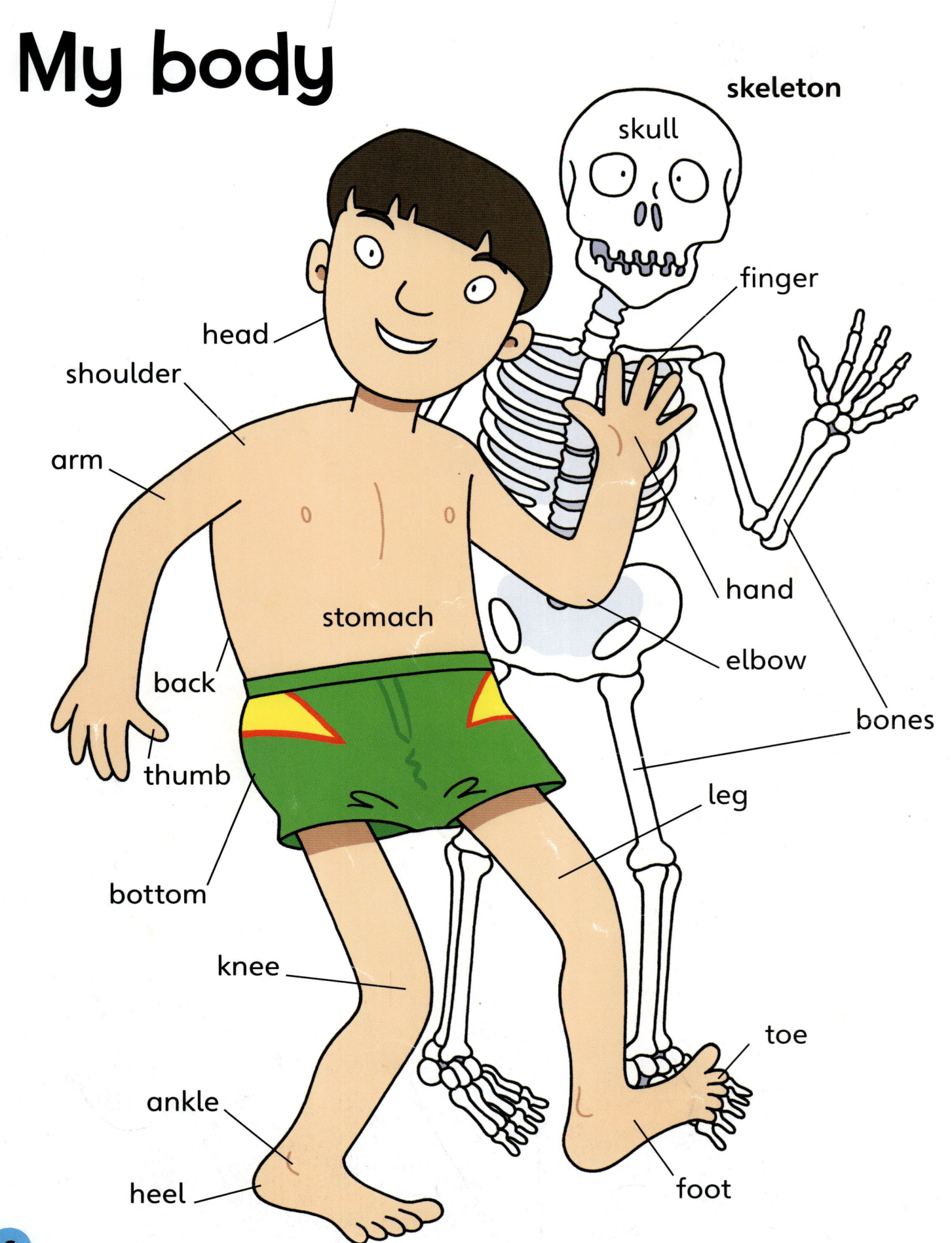

Clothes

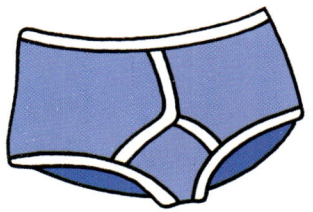 underpants

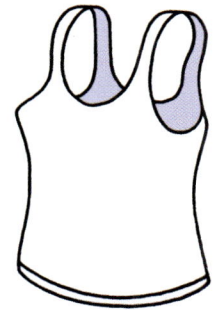 vest

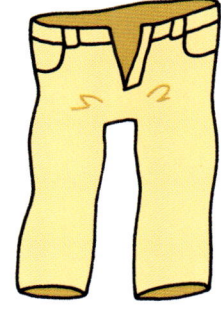 trousers

 slippers

 pyjamas

 dressing gown

 shirt

 shoes

 dress

 tie

 necklace

 ring

Clothes

Kitchen

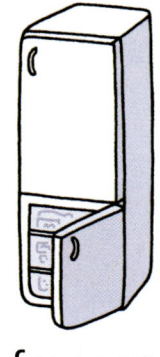
freezer

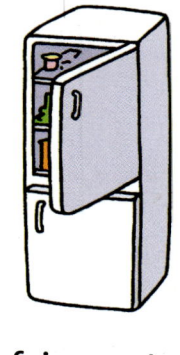
refrigerator

grater

oven

cupboard

radio

microwave oven

sink

Dinner time

vase flowers

Living Room

clock

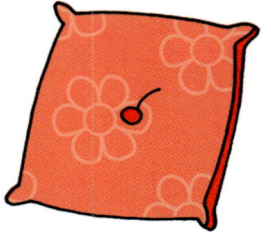
cushion

carpet

ornament

television

fireplace

sofa

lamp

picture

armchair

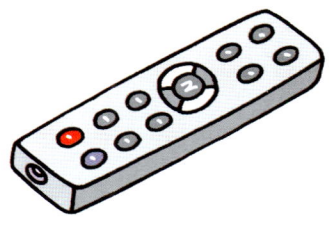
photograph

remote control

Garden

pond

greenhouse

washing line

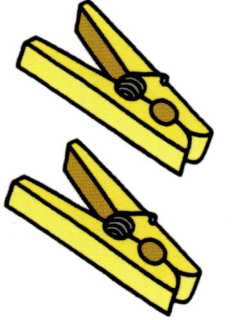
pegs

tree

watering can

bush

flowers

barbecue

hedge

worm

vegetable patch

flower pot

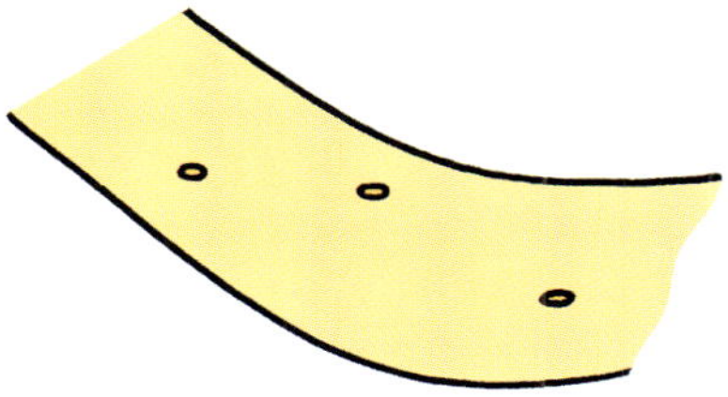

snail

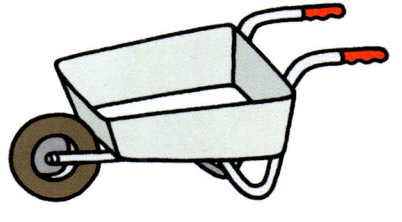
wheelbarrow

path

In the tool shed

Fruit

banana

cherries

pineapple

apple

strawberry

lime

lemon

orange

pumpkin

mango

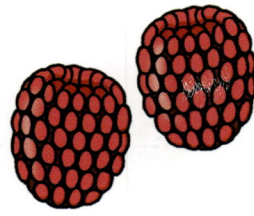
raspberries

avocado

tomato

kiwi fruit

Drinks

Food

sausages

chicken

fish

meat

garlic

cheese

bread

eggs

butter

yoghurt

bacon

ice cream

pasta

cereal

rice

Vegetables

potatoes

carrots

cabbage

green beans

onion

mushroom

sweetcorn

lettuce

cucumber

peppers

cauliflower

peas

courgette

parsnip

spring onions

aubergine

beetroot

broccoli

Things for school

pencil case

lunchbox

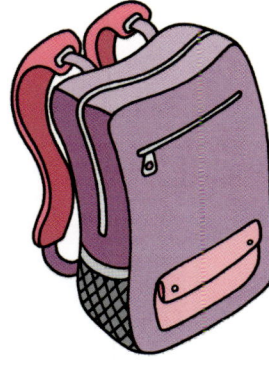
school bag

pencil

dictionary

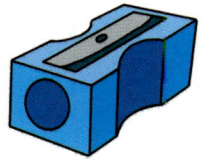
pencil sharpener

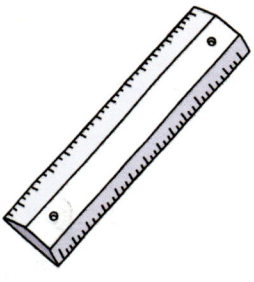
ruler

pencil crayons

eraser

calculator

pens

notebook

Lessons

 mathematics

 music

 art

 English

 ICT

 drama

 science

 history

 PE

 geography

 cookery

 religious education

Shapes

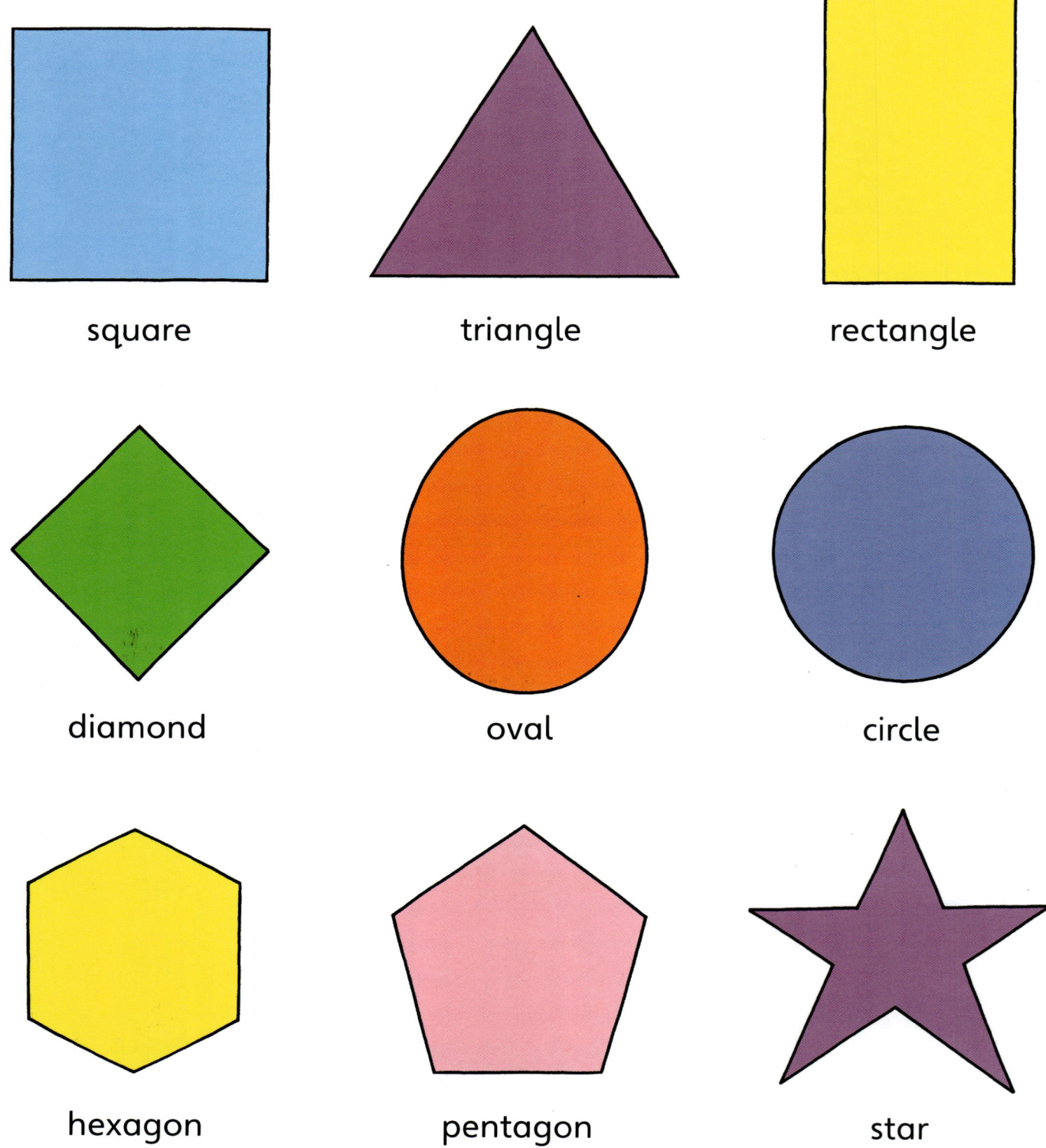

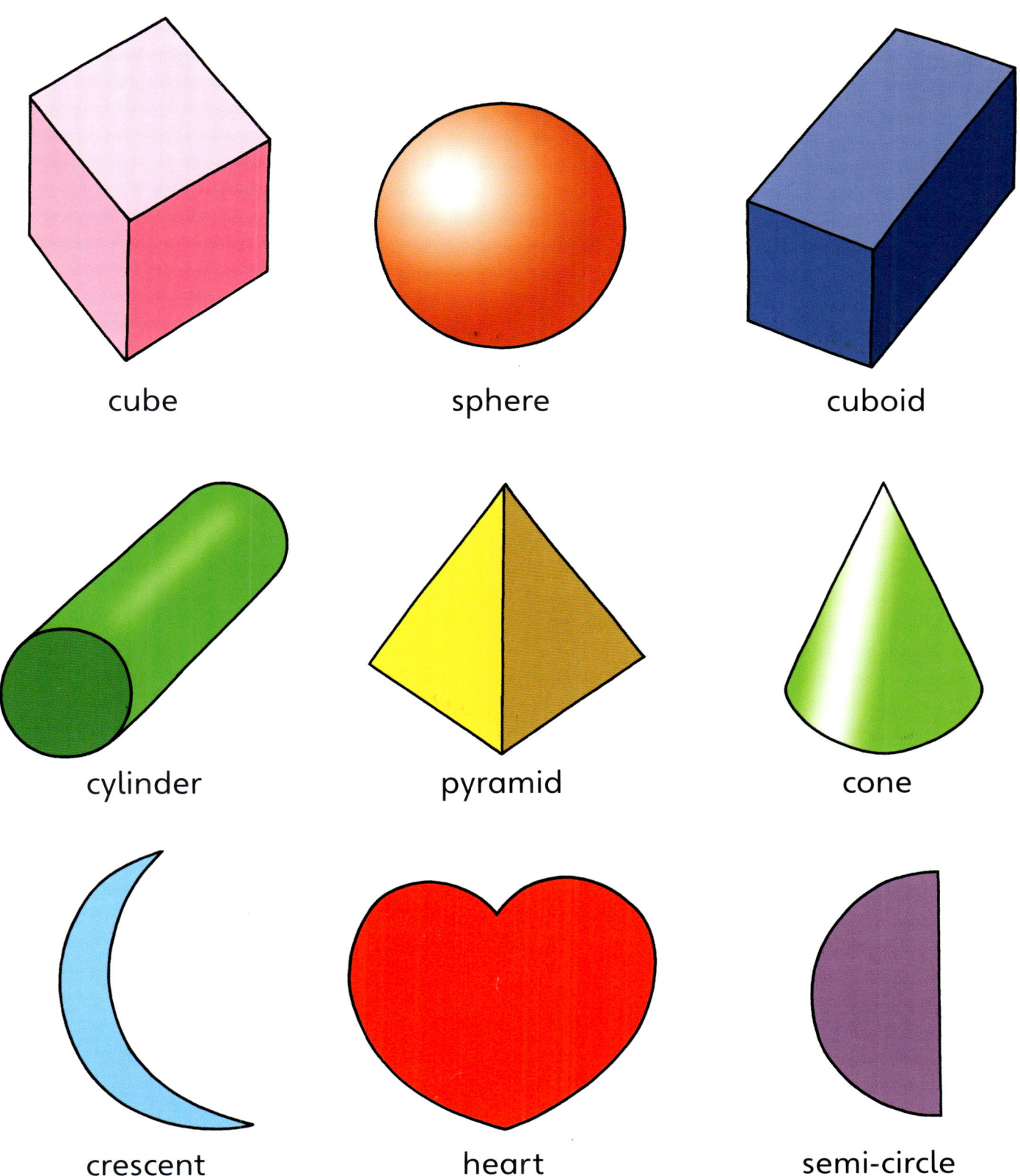

Camping

tent

rucksack

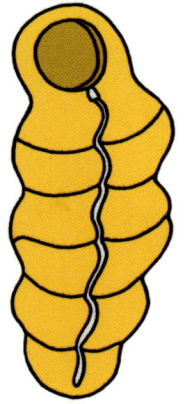
sleeping bag

torch

camping stove

campfire

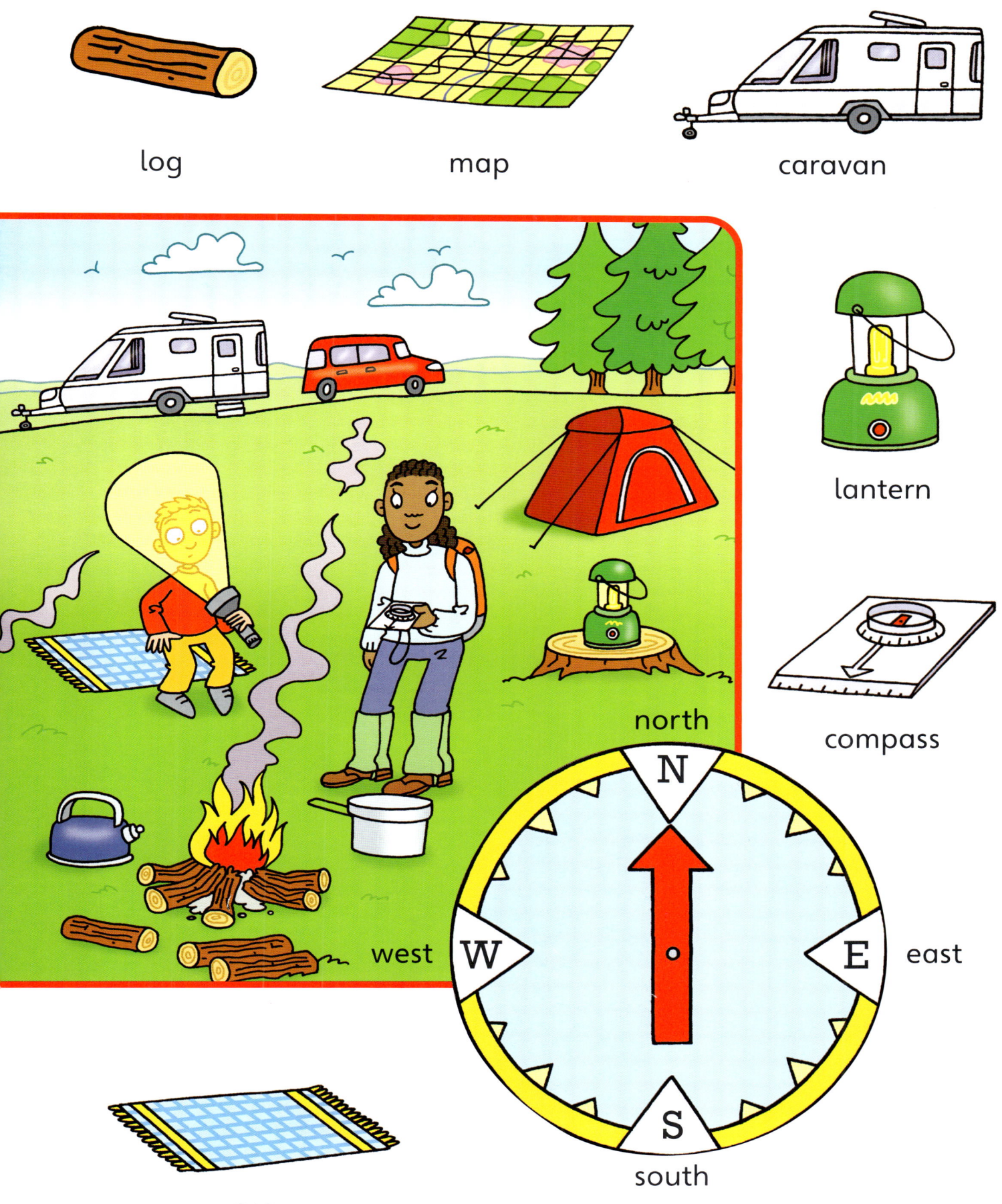

On the farm

sheepdog

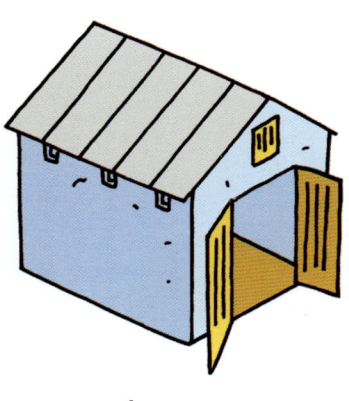
barn

field

farmer

fence

scarecrow

trailer

combine harvester

stable

tractor

crops

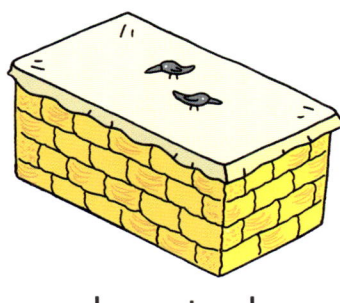
haystack

plough

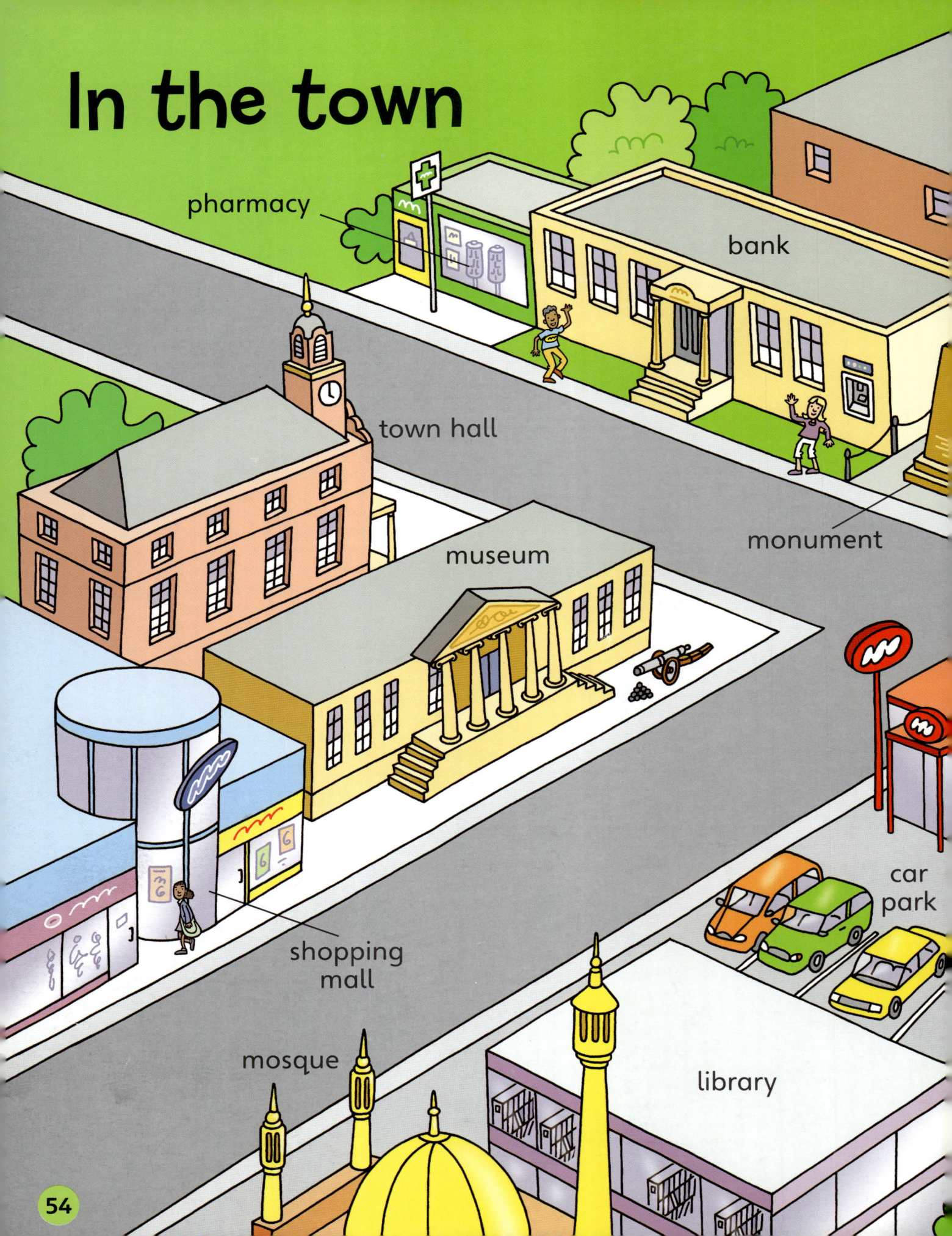

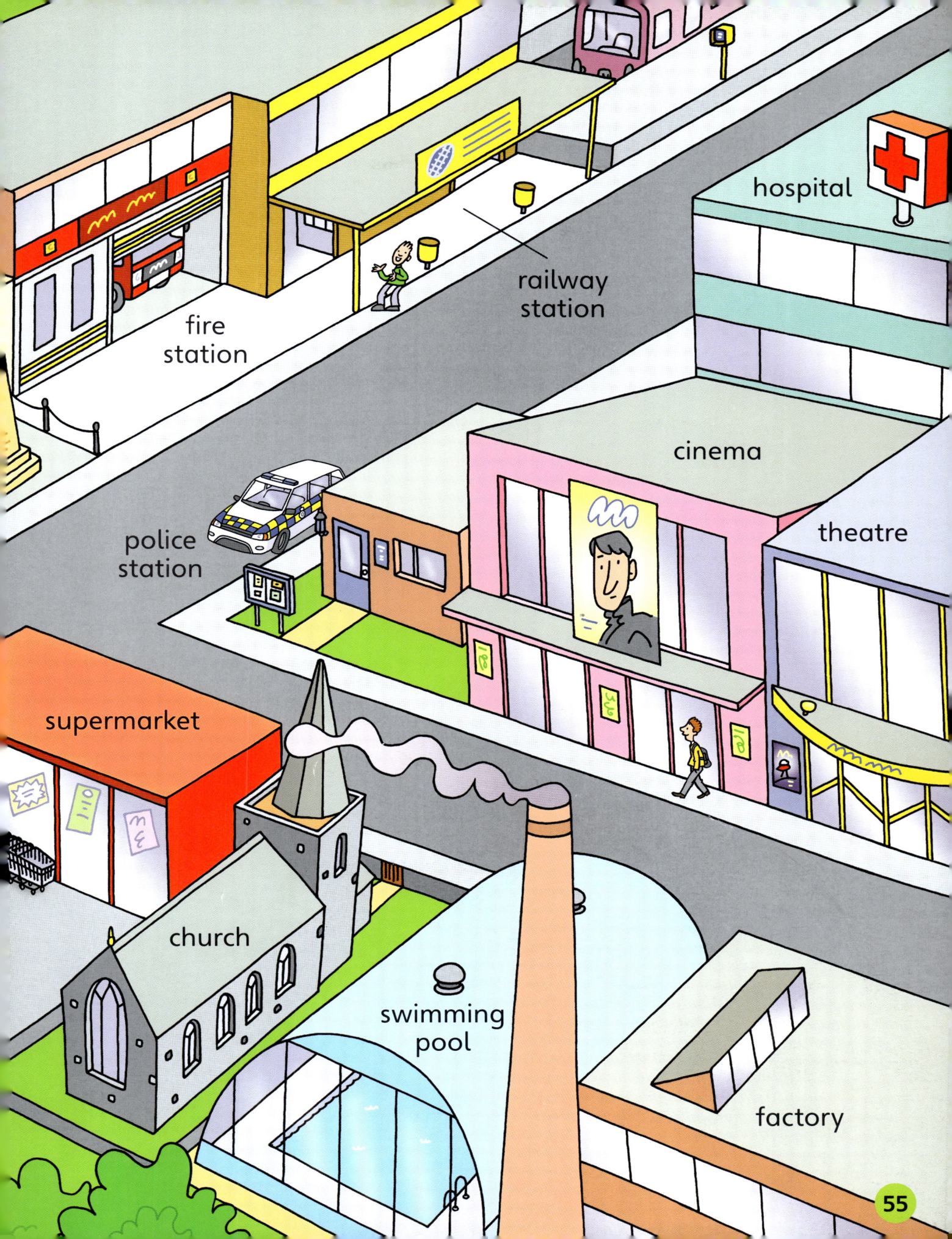

In the street

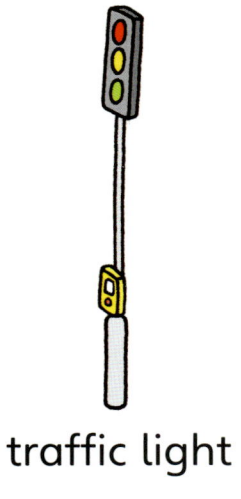 traffic light

 bus stop

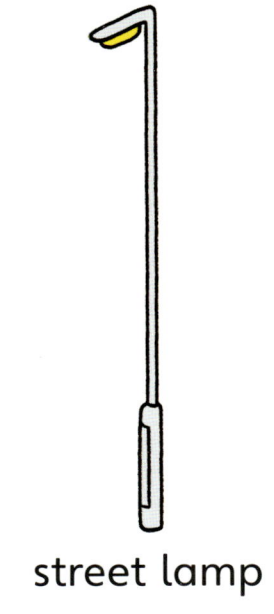 street lamp

 newspaper kiosk

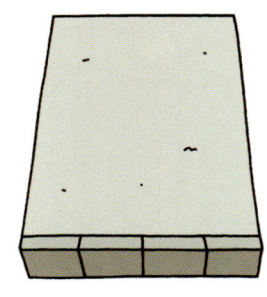 pavement

 taxi

 postbox

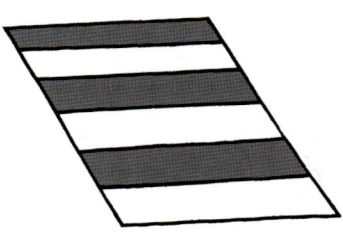 pedestrian crossing

 hairdressing salon

 butcher

 bakery

 florist

traffic warden — market — bicycle rack

Land transport

bus · bicycle · motorbike

car · tram · train

police car · fire engine · truck

Sea and air transport

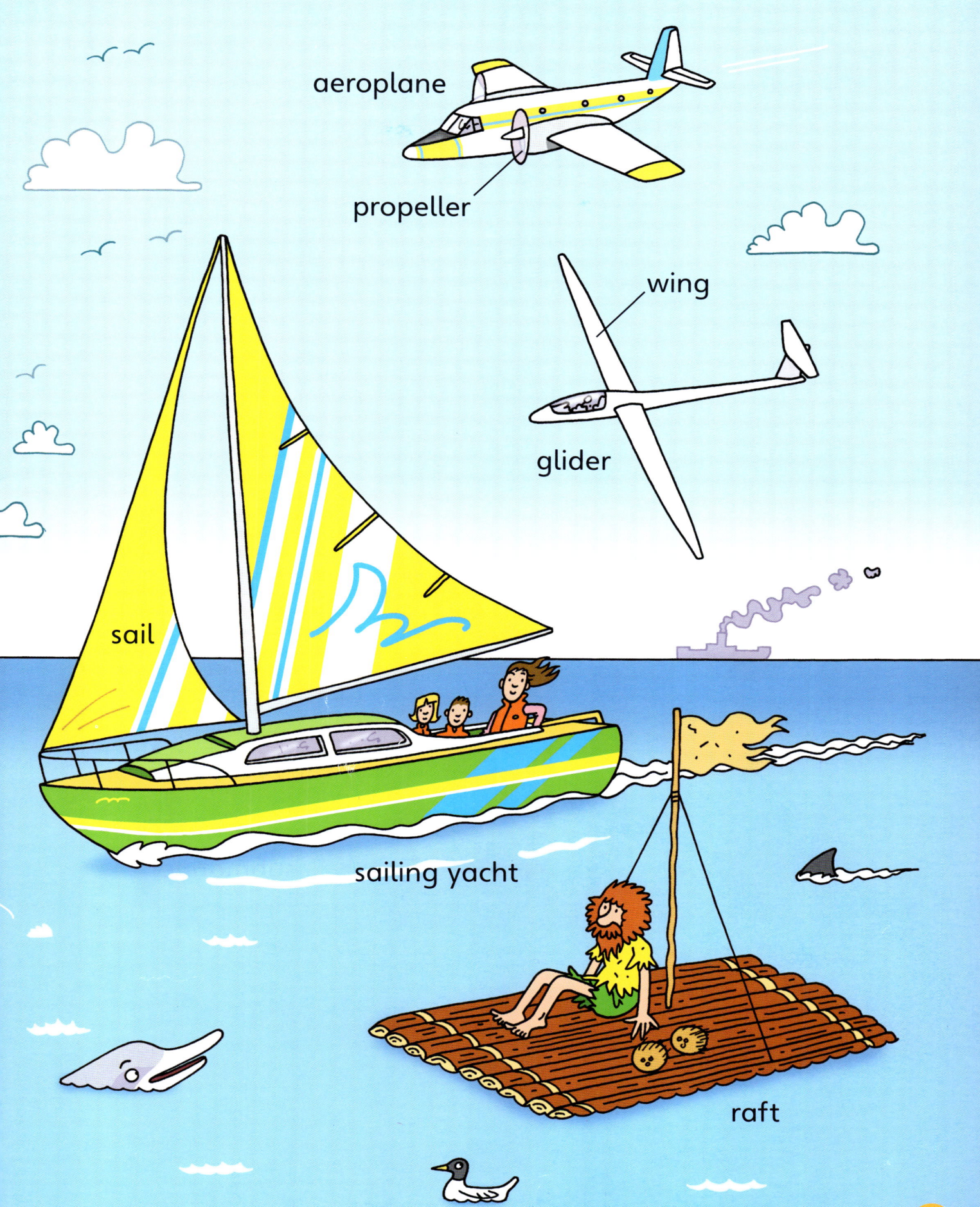

Jobs

archaeologist

hairdresser

firefighter

scientist

plumber

mechanic

pilot

astronaut

policeman

vet

postman

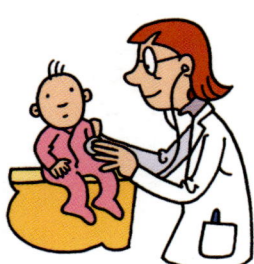
doctor

nurse

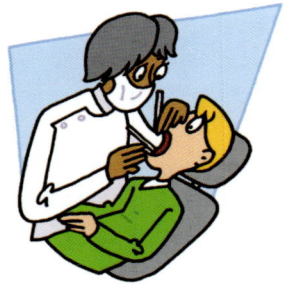
dentist

 footballer

 athlete

 musician

 actor

 optician

 builder

 lawyer

 judge

 chef

 soldier

 diver

 author

 journalist

 photographer

 shop assistant

Sports

football

skiing

cricket

snowboarding

golf

tennis

Sports equipment

airport

hotel

At the beach

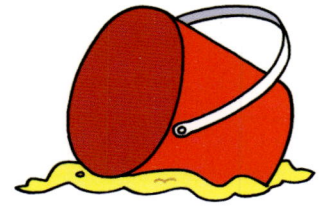
bucket

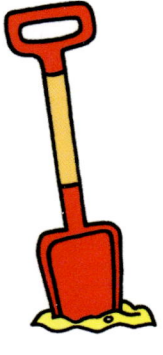
spade

sandcastle

windsurfer

ice lolly

rockpool

cliff

lifeguard

shell

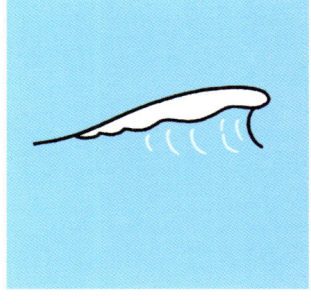
wave

sea

pier

seaweed

deckchair

surfer

Pets and their homes

Insects and bugs

caterpillar

butterfly

wasp

bee

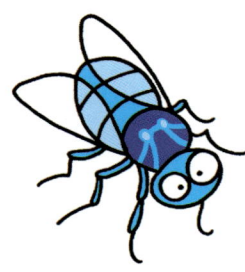
fly

moth

grasshopper

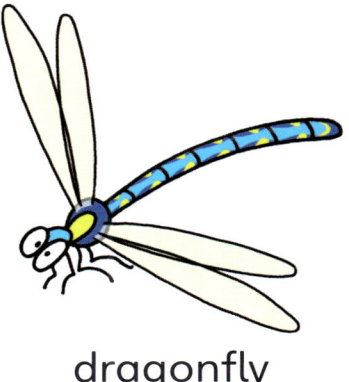
dragonfly

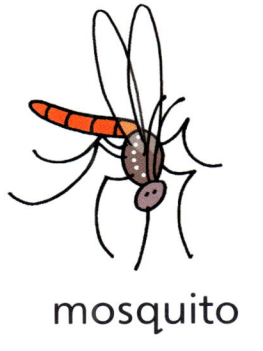
mosquito

ladybird

spider

ant

Wild animals

bear

lion

monkey

tiger

gorilla

giraffe

crocodile

hippopotamus

orangutan

Sealife

Farm animals

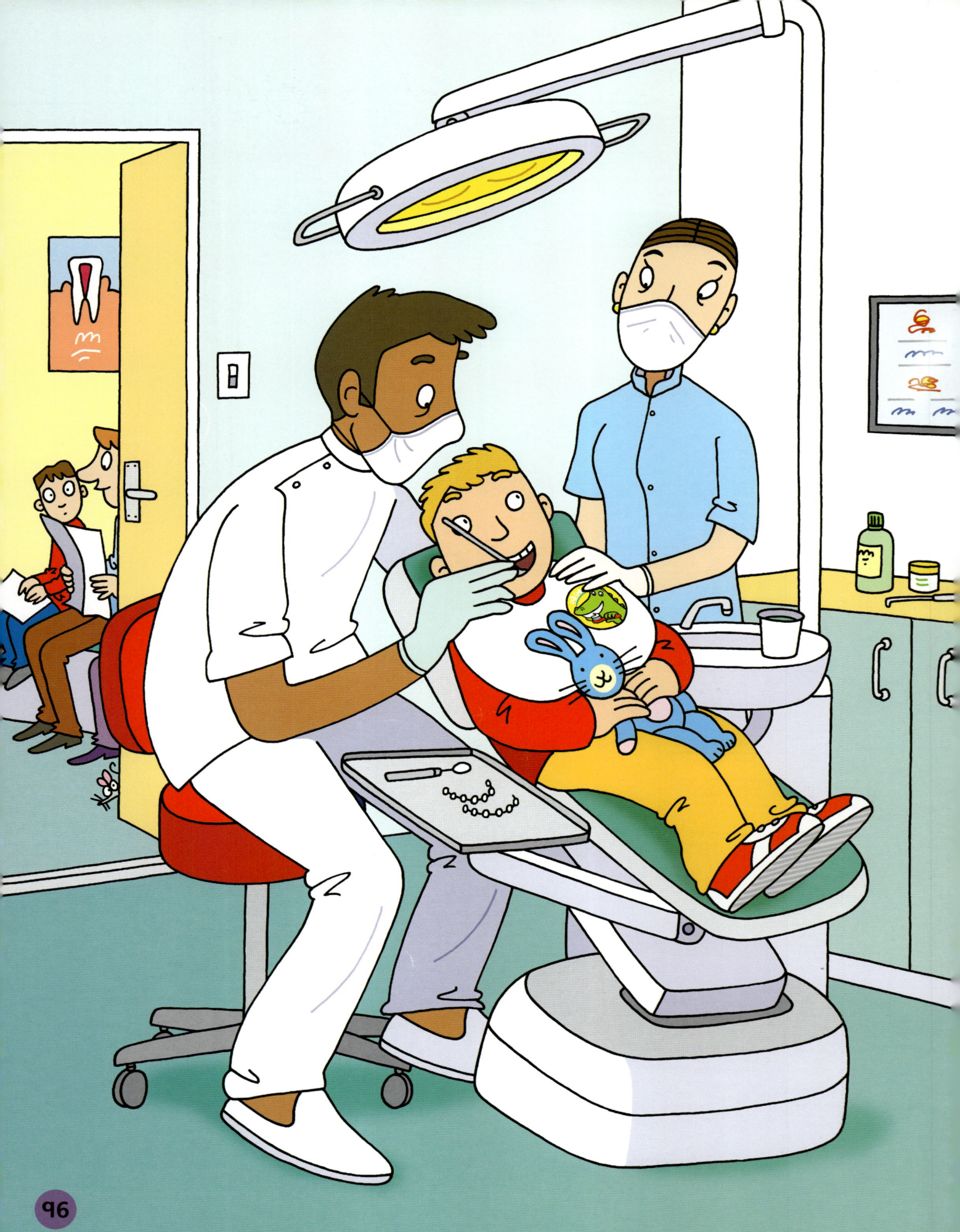

Going to the dentist

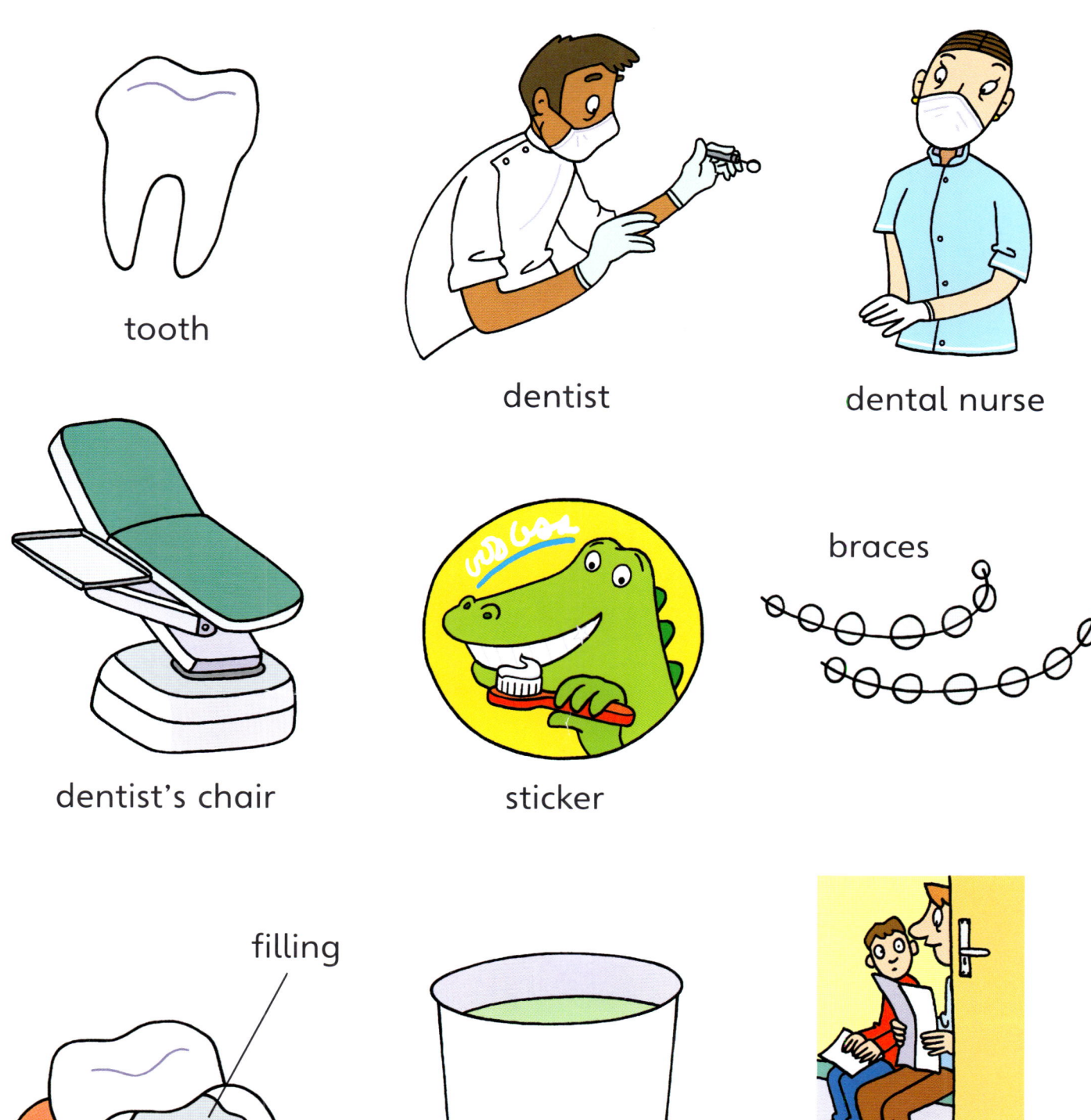

In a restaurant

At the supermarket

Days of the week

Monday

Tuesday

Wednesday

Thursday

Friday

Saturday

Sunday

Months of the year

Weather

windy

rainy

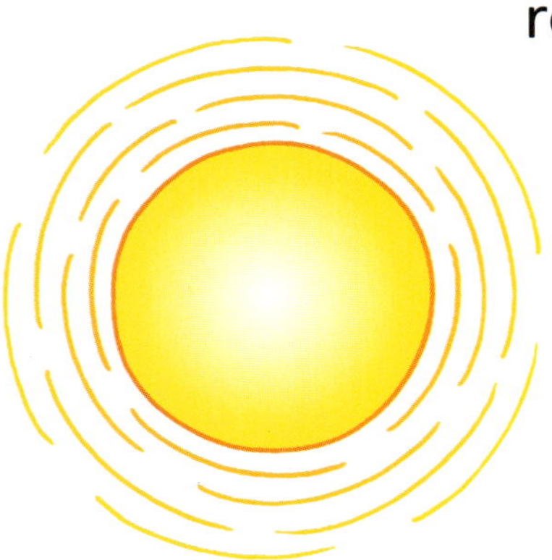

sunny

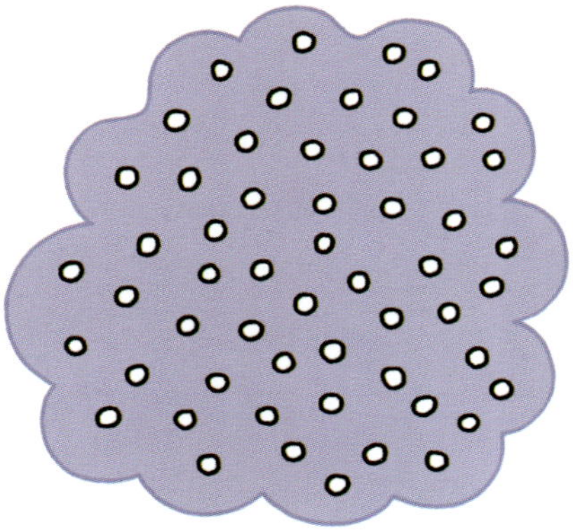

snowy

foggy

cloudy

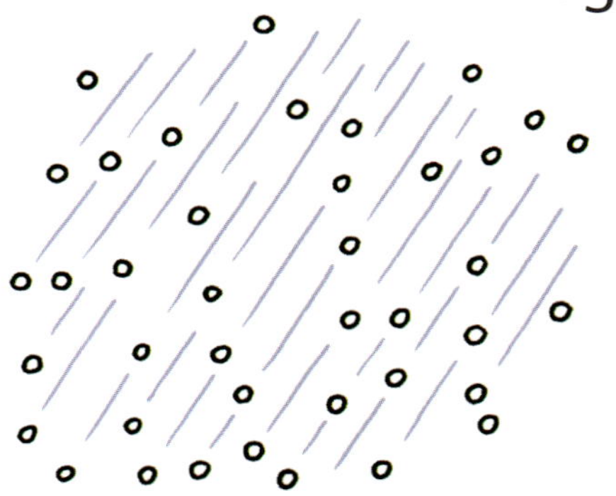

hail

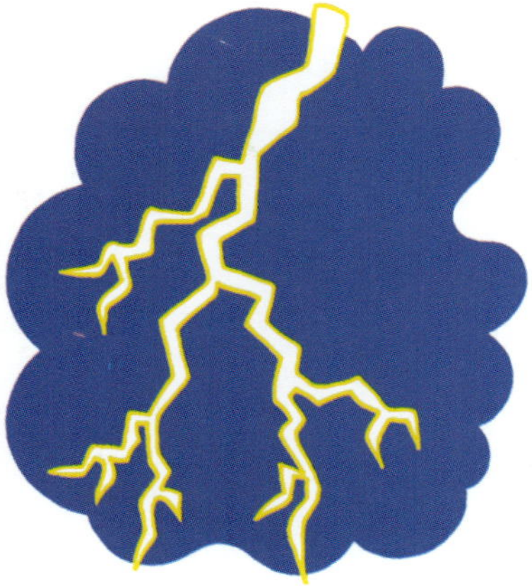

lightning

rainbow

tornado

Seasons

spring

summer

autumn

winter

Telling the time

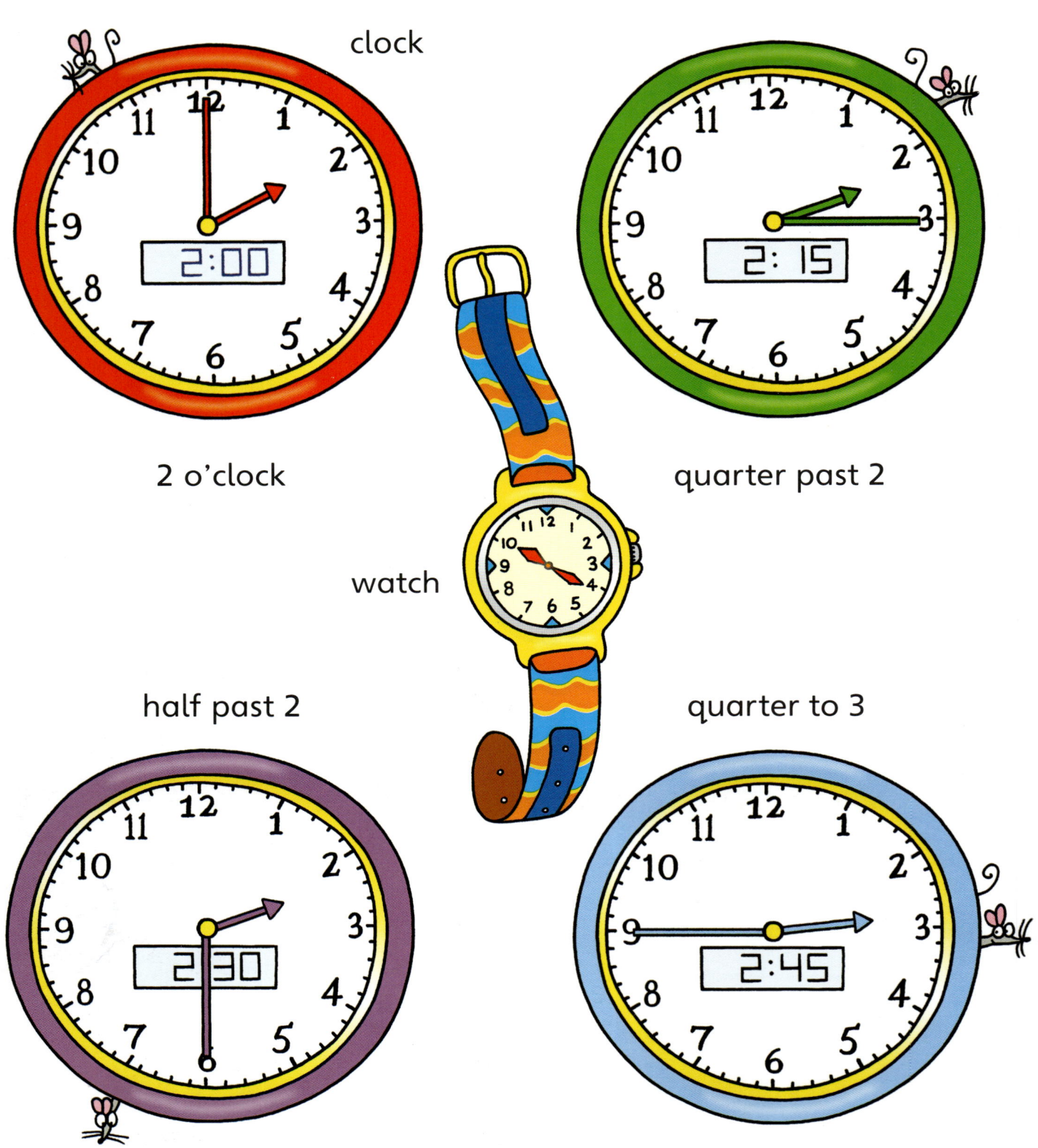

The time of the day

morning midday afternoon

evening night midnight

Opposites

Out in space

stars

Uranus

Jupiter

Neptune

rocket

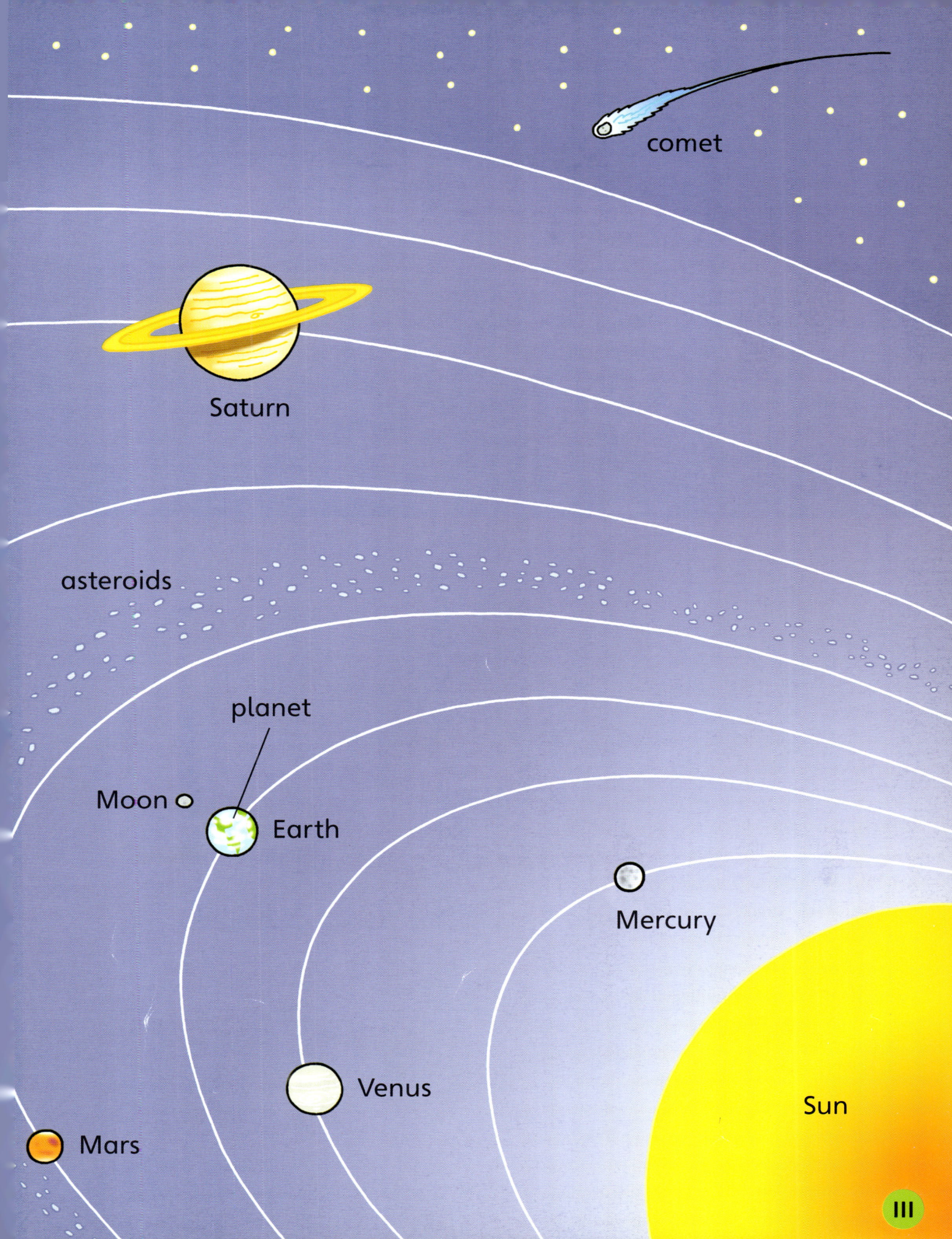

Dinosaurs

Tyrannosaurus rex

Stegosaurus

Diplodocus

Pterodactyl

Triceratops

Ancient Egypt

- pyramid
- Sphinx
- pharaoh
- mummy

Ancient Greece

- theatre
- mosaic
- pottery
- Olympic games

Fairy tales

palace
fairy
wand
king
queen
carriage
prince
princess
crown

116

Adventures

flying carpet

pirate

castle

sword

treasure chest

alien

giant

knight

genie

mermaid

troll

dragon

monster

island

Festivals

Chinese New Year

fireworks

carnival

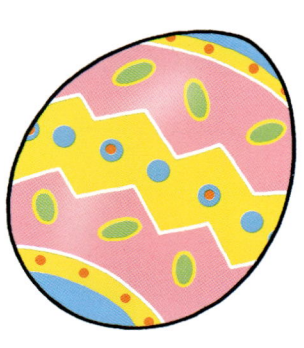
Easter egg

Easter

parade

Ramadan

Eid

Diwali

Halloween

menorah

Hanukkah

Christmas

Christmas tree

Father Christmas

reindeer

sleigh

Numbers

1 one   2 two   3 three   4 four

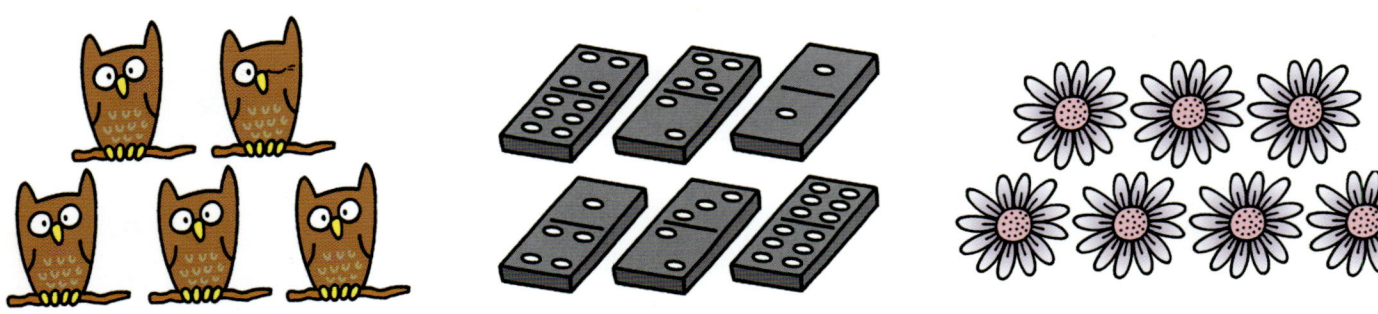

5 five   6 six   7 seven

8 eight

9 nine

10 ten

11 eleven

12 twelve

13 thirteen

14 fourteen

15 fifteen

16 sixteen

17 seventeen

18 eighteen

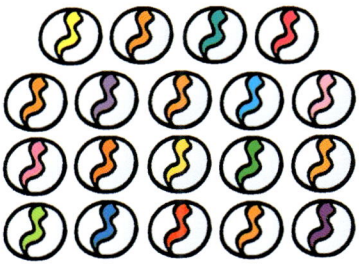

19 nineteen

20 twenty

Numbers

30 thirty

40 forty

50 fifty

60 sixty

70 seventy

80 eighty

90 ninety

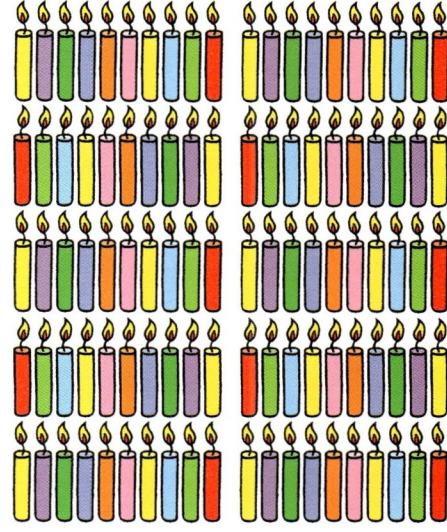

100 one hundred

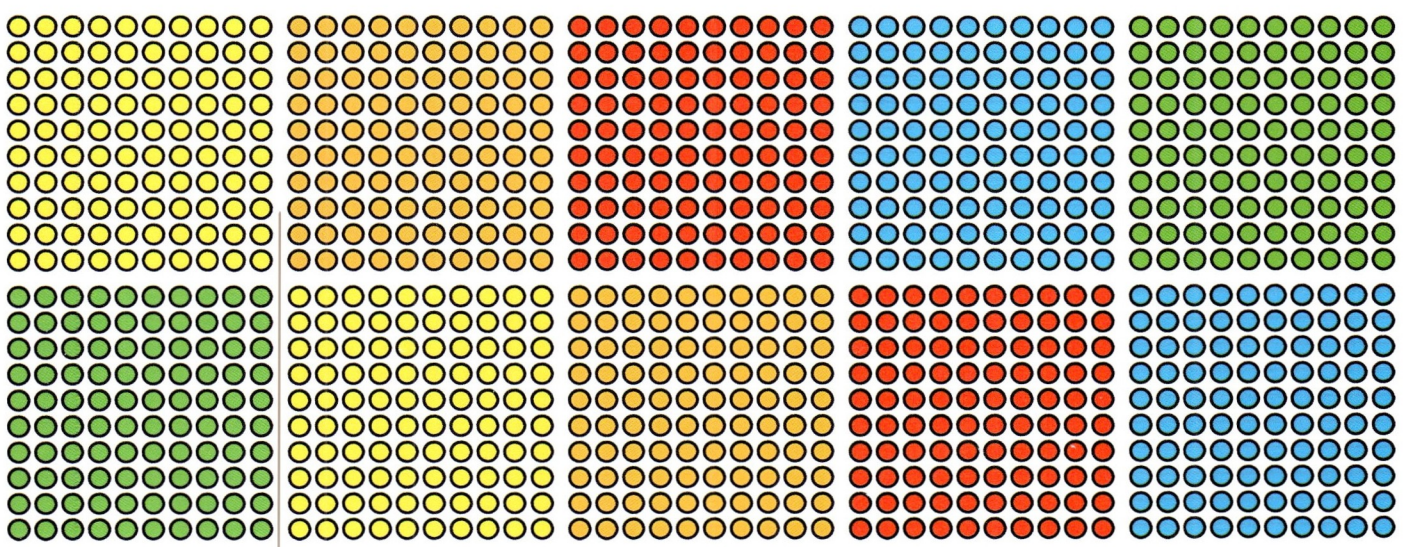

1000
one thousand

apple bicycle cave d
castle onion laptop
glove house insect f
pizza music footbal
kayak drums parade
frog garden pumpki
igloo helicopter kite
rainbow truck blue
dolphin market tra
star bridge horse st
yacht xylophone tr